Amphibian Monitoring in the Greater Yellowstone Network—Project Report 2008 and 2009

Yellowstone and Grand Teton National Parks

Natural Resource Data Series NPS/GRYN/NRDS—2010/072

Debra A. Patla

Herpetology Laboratory
Department of Biological Sciences
Idaho State University
Pocatello, Idaho 83209

Current address
Northern Rockies Conservation Cooperative
P.O. Box 2705
Jackson, WY 83001

Cathie Jean

National Park Service
Greater Yellowstone Network
2327 University Way, Suite 2
Bozeman, Montana 95715

August 2010

U.S. Department of the Interior
National Park Service
Natural Resource Program Center
Fort Collins, Colorado

The National Park Service, Natural Resource Program Center publishes a range of reports that address natural resource topics of interest and applicability to a broad audience in the National Park Service and others in natural resource management, including scientists, conservation and environmental constituencies, and the public.

The Natural Resource Data Series is intended for timely release of basic data sets and data summaries. Care has been taken to assure accuracy of raw data values, but a thorough analysis and interpretation of the data has not been completed. Consequently, the initial analyses of data in this report are provisional and subject to change.

All manuscripts in the series receive the appropriate level of peer review to ensure that the information is scientifically credible, technically accurate, appropriately written for the intended audience, and designed and published in a professional manner.

Data in this report were collected and analyzed using methods based on established, peer-reviewed protocols and were analyzed and interpreted within the guidelines of the protocols.

Views, statements, findings, conclusions, recommendations, and data in this report do not necessarily reflect view and policies of the National Park Service, U.S. Department of the Interior. Mention of trade names or commercial products does not constitute endorsement or recommendation for use by the National Park Service.

This report is available from the Greater Yellowstone Network (http://science.nature.nps.gov/im/units/gryn/index.cfm), the Greater Yellowstone Science Learning Center (http://www.greateryellowstonescience.org/subproducts/79/7) and the Natural Resource Publications Management website (http://www.nature.nps.gov/publications/NRPM).

Please cite this publication as:

Patla, D. A., and C. Jean. 2010. Amphibian monitoring in the Greater Yellowstone Network— Project report 2008 and 2009: Yellowstone and Grand Teton National Parks. Natural Resource Data Series NPS/GRYN/NRDS—2010/072. National Park Service, Fort Collins, Colorado.

NPS 101/105472, 136/105472, August 2010

Contents

Page

Figures.. v

Tables vi

Acknowledgements vii

Executive Summary viii

1 Introduction.. 1

    1.1 Background of the program 1

    1.2 Conceptual model 2

    1.3 The ARMI conceptual approach.. 3

    1.4 Objectives 4

2 Methods... 5

    2.1 Study area 5

    2.2 Sampling scheme 6

    2.3 Amphibian surveys 7

    2.4 Potential breeding sites within catchments.. 8

    2.5 Boreal toad monitoring 9

    2.6 Data analysis.. 11

    2.7 Potential breeding site data analysis 12

    2.8 Boreal toad data analysis 12

3 Results... 13

    3.1 Catchments sampled and breeding sites surveyed.. 13

    3.2 Amphibian occupancy and detectability.. 16

    3.3 Breeding Sites.. 16

    3.4 Boreal toads, supplementary monitoring... 17

3.5 Amphibian disease surveillance monitoring... 17

4 Discussion.. 19

5 Literature Cited... 21

Appendix I: Boreal toad breeding areas... 25

Figures

Page

Figure 1. Conceptual model: factors affecting the location, size, and quality of wetlands may affect the distribution and number of amphibian breeding populations. 3

Figure 2. Catchments selected for long-term amphibian monitoring in Grand Teton and Yellowstone national parks. All potential amphibian breeding sites within these 40 catchments are targeted; 32 catchments in Yellowstone, 8 in Grand Teton.... 5

Figure 3. Boreal toads breeding at Indian Pond in Yellowstone National Park 9

Figure 4. Boreal toad breeding areas in Yellowstone and Grand Teton (triangles). Breeding sites within 500 m of each other have been clustered as "toad breeding areas" for monitoring. A total of 42 breeding areas have been identified to date, six of which occur within catchments selected for the long-term monitoring project. 10

Tables

Page

Table 1. Number of catchments per access class, habitat class, and basin sampled for long-term monitoring in 2008.. 6

Table 2. Number of catchments per access class, habitat class, and basin sampling for long-term monitoring from 2009 forward. 7

Table 3. Results of amphibian monitoring in 2005–2009. Total numbers of catchments and sites surveyed per basin, and the number of catchments and sites containing breeding sites for amphibian species. 14

Table 4. Results of monitoring in 31 catchments that were surveyed each year, 2007, 2008, and 2009: number of sites surveyed, sites visited but found dry or too shallow for amphibian breeding, and number of active breeding sites per species in this set of catchments. 15

Table 5. Provisional catchment-level occupancy and detection rates from 2008 monitoring data. Occupancy estimates were calculated using a model that allowed occupancy to vary by habitat strata (high+medium and low) and assumed constant detectability across strata........................ 16

Table 6. Provisional catchment-level occupancy and detection rates from 2009 monitoring data. Occupancy estimates were calculated using a model that allowed occupancy to vary by habitat strata (high+medium and low) and assumed constant detectability across strata........................ 16

Table 9. Tally of site visits per year, 2006–2009. 17

Acknowledgements

We extend our thanks and appreciation to the following people and agencies:

Funding for this project was provided by the National Park Service Greater Yellowstone Inventory and Monitoring Network (GRYN) and the U.S. Geological Survey (USGS). In 2009, funding for surveys was supplemented by the Yellowstone National Park Amphibian Disease Surveillance Project, headed by Sophie St-Hilaire (Idaho State University). The principal investigators are Charles R. Peterson (Idaho State University) and P. Stephen Corn (USGS). At GRYN, Rob Daley provided database management and technical support. Stacey Ostermann-Kelm reviewed and improved this report. Robert Bennetts, who left GRYN in 2007, was a primary architect of the sample design and initial monitoring protocol for this project. Dr. Bennetts contributed directly to this report as we carried over his figures from the 2006 annual report. William Gould advanced the project thorough evaluation of sampling design and recommendations, and this report benefits from sections of the 2007 annual report, which Dr. Gould co-authored. USGS provided technical support for data collection and the database (Blake Hossack, Chris Brown, and Donn Holms). Idaho State University administered field crew employment in 2008; Big Sky Institute provided this service in 2009 (our thanks to Diane Eagleson and Todd Kipfer). Field crew members in 2008 and 2009 were Robert Bragg, Dennis Kaleta, Scott Martin, Ashley Spenceley, Janene Colby, Mary Greenblatt, Eric Hupperts, Britt Ousterhout, and Christine Rollinson; also Sara Dykman, Paul Scarr, Nathan Muhn, and Lindy Mullen (USGS), Lance Haynes (Yellowstone), and Haley Smith and David Cockerill (Grand Teton). Expert volunteers donated time and travel costs to help with catchment surveys and toad monitoring: Char and Dave Corkran, Laura Trunk, and Laura Guderyahn. Fisheries and Aquatic Resources (Yellowstone) supplemented the field work effort on the Northern Range in 2008: Todd Koel, Jeff Arnold, Hilary Billman, and others. Katy Duffy (Yellowstone) assisted the project by monitoring toads and contributing amphibian observations. David Green of the USGS National Wildlife Health Center provided diagnostic services for collected specimens. Sue Consolo-Murphy (Grand Teton) and Dusty Perkins (Northern Colorado Plateau Network) reviewed this report and provided valuable comments. Personnel from Yellowstone and Grand Teton supported multiple aspects of permits and logistics, particularly Christie Hendrix, Christine Smith, Stacey Gunther, Austin Murphy, Eric Reinertson, Margie Fey, and Pat Perotti in Yellowstone; Susan Wolff, Steve Cain, Sarah Dewey, and Cindy O'Neill in Grand Teton.

Executive Summary

The national parks within the Greater Yellowstone Ecosystem (GYE) provide an opportunity to monitor amphibians within a relatively intact ecosystem, at spatial and temporal scales that can provide important insights about the status of regional amphibian populations and global declines of amphibians. The Greater Yellowstone Network (GRYN) amphibian monitoring program is the only long-term amphibian monitoring program in the GYE that consistently looks at multiple sites across the ecosystem. The goal of this program is to estimate occupancy rates for the reproductive component of native amphibian species, incorporating the dynamics of wetland sites that provide potential breeding habitat. Annual measures of amphibian occurrence and wetland suitability allow trends in amphibian populations to be considered in context of the available habitat. This work will provide managers and the public with information about the status of a class of native fauna in the Parks and wetland habitat trends that may be strongly related to climate change.

Based on visual encounter surveys at 40 and 37 catchments, occupancy rates for 2008 and 2009 are 0.16 and 0.09 for tiger salamanders (*Ambystoma mavortium*), 0.49 and 0.47 for boreal chorus frogs (*Pseudacris maculata*), 0.45 and 0.42 for Columbia spotted frogs (*Rana luteiventris*) and 0.06 and 0.05 for boreal toads (*Anaxyrus boreas boreas*). The percentage of wetland sites suitable for amphibian breeding increased in response to increases in precipitation in 2008 and 2009 compared to earlier years. No bullfrogs or leopard frogs were detected at any sites. Six new boreal toad breeding sites have been located from 2005 to 2009 as part of the catchment monitoring. Analysis of multi-year trends in amphibian occupancy is in progress, with the intention of completing a paper for publication in 2011.

Previous work has stated that 3 amphibian species (Columbia spotted frogs, boreal chorus frogs, and tiger salamanders) are considered common and widespread in Yellowstone and Grand Teton. Based on more sampling across different quality habitat, their occurrence is better stated as widespread throughout the two parks, but in limited and unevenly distributed suitable wetland breeding habitat. The increase in amphibian breeding sites between 2007 and 2008 demonstrates the ability of native amphibians to respond to improved moisture conditions with increased breeding efforts. However, it also suggests their vulnerability if climate change results in extended periods of unrelieved drought, shrinking wetlands, and larger proportions of available water diverted for human uses.

1 Introduction

Concerns about amphibians have escalated since population declines became apparent in diverse areas around the world in the 1980s (Collins and Storfer 2003; Wake and Vredenburg 2008). Systematic examinations have revealed that in some regions, including North America, rapid declines probably began around the middle of the 20th century, with the rate of decline increasing in the 1990s (Houlahan et al. 2000; Alford et al. 2001). Worldwide, 32% of amphibian species are now threatened with extinction, while 43% exhibit some form of population decrease (Stuart et al. 2004). Amidst the rapid and general decline in global biodiversity, amphibian population extinctions and declines are particularly alarming because they are occurring not only where habitat has been lost, but also in natural, protected areas. The six leading hypotheses for explaining amphibian declines are land use changes causing habitat loss and degradation, infectious diseases, global change (climate warming and increased ultraviolet radiation), toxic chemicals (e.g., pesticides), invasive species, and over-exploitation of wild amphibians for food or the pet trade (Collins and Storfer 2003). Of these hypotheses, widespread land use changes, toxic chemicals, and commercial exploitation are minimized or unlikely to occur at Grand Teton and Yellowstone National Parks. Invasive species of potential concern include non-native fish, New Zealand mud snail, and bullfrogs. A recent publication attributed amphibian declines on the Northern Range of Yellowstone to climate change (McMenamin et al. 2008). A recent, global concern is the amphibian disease chytridiomycosis, caused by a species of parasitic fungus first identified in 1998 (Cascon et al. 2007) and likely the cause of amphibian declines in Colorado (Muths et al. 2003). The pathogenic fungus is widespread in amphibian populations of northwest Wyoming (Muths et al. 2008), and lethal outbreaks of the endemic amphibian disease, ranavirus, have also been discovered at multiple sites in Yellowstone and Grand Teton. Many of the world's rapid amphibian population declines are poorly understood and likely have complex causes involving multiple factors. Long-term monitoring of amphibian populations across Grand Teton and Yellowstone provides an opportunity to observe trends that may not be apparent at local scales or in areas where there are more direct human influences on habitat quality. The program is partially supported by the U.S. Geological Survey (USGS), and it complements similar amphibian monitoring projects on Department of Interior lands in Colorado, Montana, and the Pacific Northwest (http://armi.usgs.gov/).

1.1 Background of the program

Yellowstone and Grand Teton National Parks have a relatively depauperate amphibian fauna compared to forested ecosystems at lower elevations and in more temperate regions. Three amphibian species are apparently widespread and locally common to abundant in Yellowstone and Grand Teton National Parks: tiger salamanders (*Ambystoma mavortium,* formerly *Ambystoma tigrinum*), boreal chorus frog (*Pseudacris maculata*), and Columbia spotted frog (*Rana luteiventris*) (amphibian nomenclature follows Crother 2008). Boreal toads (*Anaxyrus boreas boreas*, formerly *Bufo boreas boreas*) are apparently now less widespread and less common than in the 1950s (Koch and Peterson 1995). Northern leopard frogs (*Lithobates pipiens,* formerly *Rana pipiens*) have vanished from Grand Teton. One nonnative species, the American bullfrog (*Lithobates catesbeianus*, formerly *Rana catesbeiana*), occurs in Grand Teton at Kelly Warm Springs.

Efforts to monitor amphibians in the GYE began at 10 sites in the 1990s by Idaho State University (ISU), the National Park Service (NPS) and the U.S. Fish and Wildlife Service. Monitoring efforts were formalized following the selection of amphibians as a vital sign by the NPS Greater Yellowstone Inventory and Monitoring Network (GRYN) (Jean et al. 2005) and a monitoring protocol was written in collaboration between the USGS Amphibian Research Monitoring Initiative (ARMI), and ISU (Amphibian Monitoring Working Group 2008). ARMI has designated the GYE as the central portion of the Great Divide Transect, a system of amphibian monitoring and research projects extending from Glacier National Park to Rocky Mountain National Park (Corn et al. 2005b). The approach to monitoring amphibians involves comprehensive, repeated amphibian breeding surveys of wetlands within small watersheds (referred to as catchments). In 2008, the monitoring methods were finalized and they represent the first year of data for which trends of all selected catchments can be analyzed. This report summarizes the field work from the 2005 to 2009, with emphasis on the two most recent field seasons.

1.2 Conceptual model

Long-term monitoring of amphibians provides insights into how well the GRYN is maintaining a significant component of biological diversity, and may help NPS managers and biologists assess the level of overall ecological condition or stress. Amphibians serve as useful indicators because they are sensitive to stressors that are of prominent concern to national park managers and the public, including climate change, diseases, contaminants, habitat alteration, and introduced nonnative species.

Amphibian populations can respond in a number of ways to these stressors and variables: occupancy and distribution patterns may change, species may disappear regionally or within administrative units, the abundance of individuals can decline or increase, outbreaks of disease and malformations may occur, and the genetic structure of populations may change. Changes in amphibian populations have consequences for ecosystems. Amphibians often occur in great local abundance, providing prey for many kinds of predators including fish, reptiles, birds, and mammals. Adult amphibians are prodigious predators, consuming insects and other invertebrates. Declines or increases in amphibians thus may alter trophic relationships, and the abundance of other animals. In terms of energy flow in ecosystems, amphibians play a unique role by transporting the high productivity of wetlands to the terrestrial environment, as tadpoles metamorphose and emerge from ponds.

All amphibian species of GRYN rely on shallow water bodies for egg deposition and larval development (Koch and Peterson 1995). Thus, factors affecting the location and size of wetlands (drought or climate change, land use, and beavers) are likely to substantially affect the distribution and number of amphibian breeding populations. Some stressors have the potential to directly affect the health, survival, and abundance of amphibians: pathogens, contaminants from both local and remote sources, UV radiation, and introduced species that compete with or prey on native amphibians (such as bullfrogs, nonnative fish, and introduced snails) or plant species that degrade wetland breeding habitat. Some environmental factors may affect amphibians directly as well as indirectly, via their impacts on wetland habitats. For example, roads can cause high mortality rates in frogs attempting to reach their seasonal breeding or wintering habitat, and roads can also cause wetland loss (fig. 1).

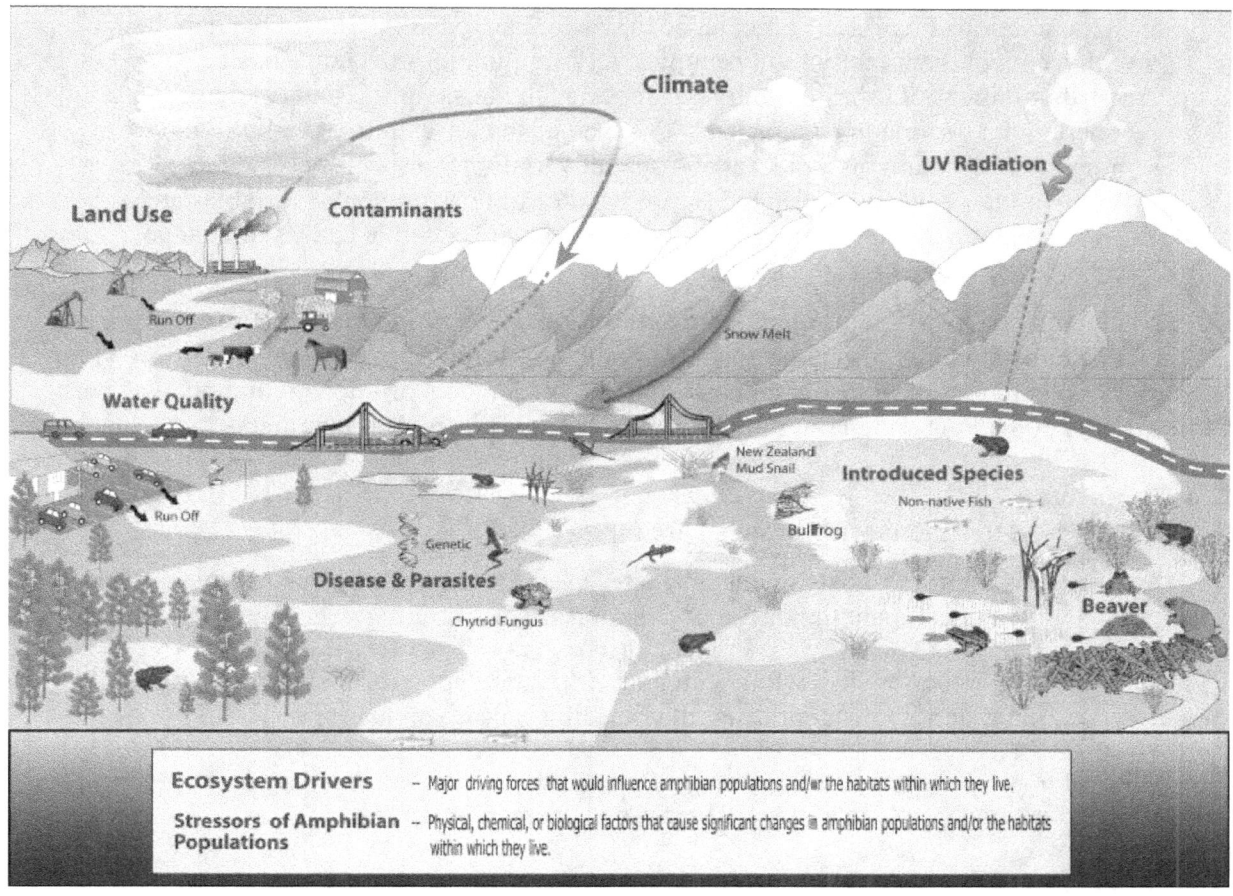

Figure 1. Conceptual model: factors affecting the location, size, and quality of wetlands may affect the distribution and number of amphibian breeding populations.

1.3 The ARMI conceptual approach

The challenge of how to monitor amphibians on extensive Department of the Interior land management units has been the subject of an integrated effort by senior USGS scientists (Corn et al. 2005a). The approach adopted for monitoring amphibians in national parks focuses on the number of populations, as opposed to changes in the size of populations. This is based on Green's (1997) framework for discerning declines:

> A decline is the condition whereby the local loss of populations across the normal range of a species so exceeds the rate at which populations maybe established, or reestablished, that there is a definite downward trend in population number.
> (Green 1997)

To assess amphibian status and trends, USGS scientists recommend monitoring changes in the proportion of area occupied based on presence-absence data, using estimation techniques that incorporate measures of detection probability and allow for testing how environmental variables affect occupancy dynamics (Corn et al. 2005a). The approach assumes:

As populations increase in abundance they should expand into available habitat with a concomitant increase in occupancy. As populations decrease in size, distributions should shrink, with fewer species in the sampling units and a concomitant decline in occupancy. Thus the occupancy estimator can provide indirect information on temporal and spatial variations in species abundance. With simultaneous monitoring at sampling sites of environmental variables and stressors that can affect amphibians, correlation with possible causes of change can be established and studied (Corn et al. 2005a).

GRYN adopted the ARMI conceptual approach for long-term amphibian monitoring in Grand Teton and Yellowstone. A formal protocol (Amphibian Monitoring Working Group 2008) for the program, including the conceptual basis and all the elements of implementation, was peer reviewed in 2008 and is undergoing minor revision to address review comments.

1.4 Objectives

The objectives of this monitoring protocol are to:

1) Estimate the proportion of catchments and sites used for breeding by each native amphibian species annually, and estimate the rate at which their use is changing over time.

2) Determine the number of sites within catchments that are potentially suitable for amphibian breeding (i.e., have standing water during the breeding season) annually.

3) For boreal toads, estimate the proportion of previously identified breeding areas that are used annually, and estimate the rate at which their use is changing over time.

The third objective is intended to supplement Objective 1, for which occupancy rates are presumed to be too low to enable reliable estimation of rates of change with inference to the entire study area, given the rarity of boreal toads relative to the other amphibian species. Current funding levels are only sufficient to address Objectives 1 and 2, but Objective 3 has been partially met through volunteer efforts.

2 Methods

2.1 Study area

Our study area is Yellowstone and Grand Teton, with inference to all portions of the parks containing shallow wetlands. Sampling units for amphibian monitoring are small portions of watersheds, referred to as catchments. Figure 2 shows the catchments that have been randomly selected for long-term monitoring.

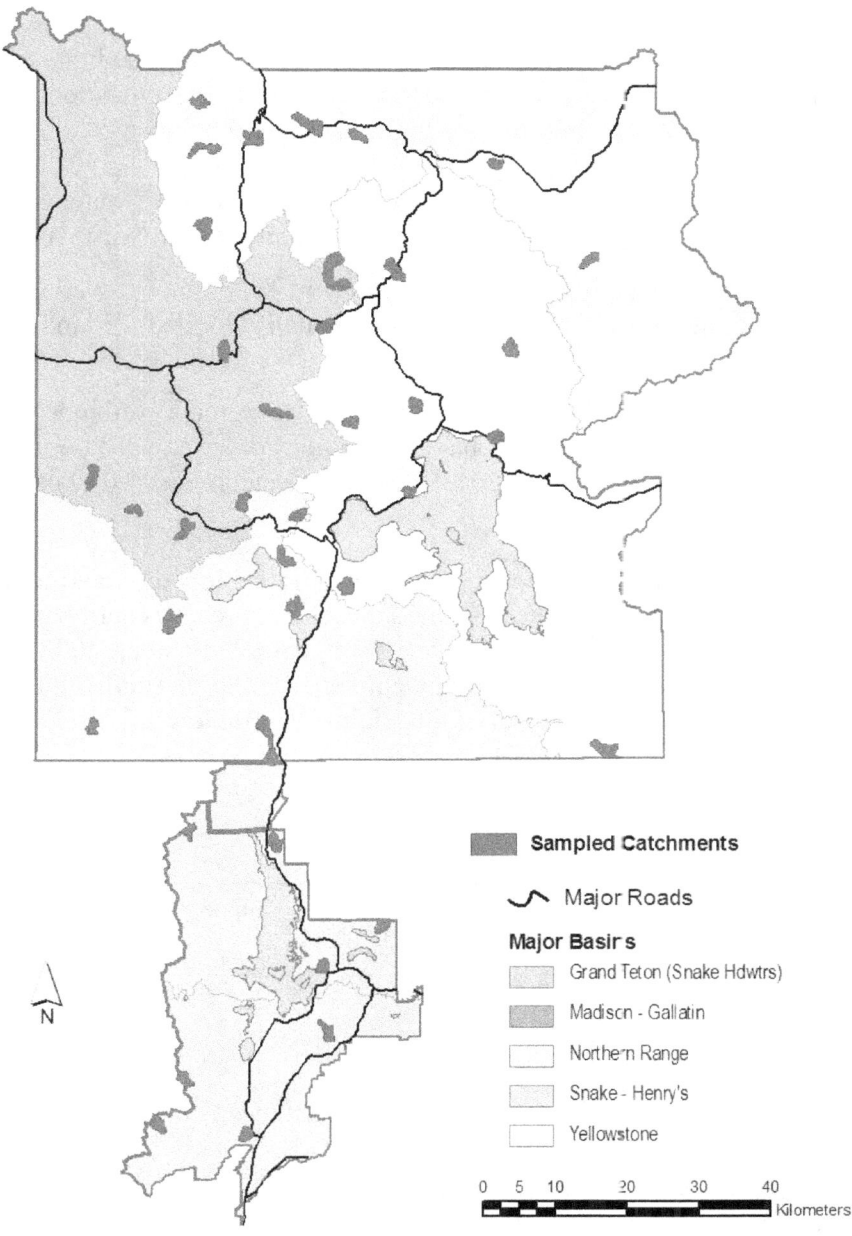

Figure 2. Catchments selected for long-term amphibian monitoring in Grand Teton and Yellowstone national parks. All potential amphibian breeding sites within these 40 catchments are targeted; 32 catchments in Yellowstone, 8 in Grand Teton

2.2 Sampling scheme

Catchment boundaries are represented in a Geographic Information System (GIS) layer created at USGS Earth Resource Observation Systems (EROS) Data Center. We used a stratified random sampling scheme to ensure spatial distribution of sampling units among the major drainage basins of Yellowstone and Grand Teton (fig. 2). To help ensure that the majority of units could be reached without extraordinary off-trail efforts during the brief field season, we used two accessibility classes ("close" or ≤ 4 km from roads and "far" or > 4 km from roads) in our allocation scheme (table 1). Since the highest quality habitat within Yellowstone and Grand Teton is limited to a small amount of the area, we sought to ensure sampling this habitat by stratifying on amphibian breeding habitat probability or quality (high, medium, and low) based on National Wetland Inventory (NWI) types and amounts within the catchment (Amphibian Monitoring Working Group 2008). We defined high, medium, and low as:

- High quality: >4 ha of semi-permanent & permanent wetlands (NWI water regime F, G, or H), AND >2 ha of seasonally flooded wetlands (NWI water regime C).

- Medium quality: >0 ha (any amount) of semi-permanent & permanent wetlands (NWI water regime F-G-H), AND >1 ha of seasonally flooded wetlands (NWI water regime C).

- Low quality: >0 ha (any amount) of semi-permanent & permanent wetlands (NWI water regime F, G, or H); OR >0 ha (any amount) of seasonally flooded wetlands (NWI water regime C) (i.e., all remaining catchments with potential surface water).

In 2006 and 2007, we visited all the selected catchments in the high and medium habitat classes but only a subset of the catchments in the low class as per our previous split panel design, which prescribed surveying catchments in this class every five years (Patla et al. 2007). Subsequent analysis of the 2007 data demonstrated that all catchments should be surveyed annually (Gould 2008), and in 2008 we surveyed the full set of 40 catchments (table 1).

Table 1. Number of catchments per access class, habitat class, and basin sampled for long-term monitoring in 2008.

		Basins						
Access Class[1]	Habitat Class[2]	Northern Range	Yellow-stone	Madison-Gallatin	Snake-Henrys Fk	Grand Teton-north[3]	Grand Teton-south	Total catchments
Close	High	2	2	2	2	1	1	10
Far	High	1	1	1	1	—	1	5
Close	Medium	2	2	2	2	1	1	10
Far	Medium	1	1	1	1	1	—	5
Close	Low	1	1	1	1	1	—	5
Far	Low	1	1	1	1	—	1	5
Total		8	8	8	8	4	4	40

[1]Based on catchment distance < or > 4 km from a road.
[2]Based on the amount and type of wetlands in each catchment identified by the National Wetland Inventory.
[3]Grand Teton is in the Snake Basin; it was divided into north and south zones to achieve better spatial representation.

Following the 2008 survey, we evaluated the time and effort requirements to survey all 40 catchments and determined that we could not reliably survey all 40 catchments annually with projected available funding, and that we needed to adjust our sample design accordingly. We discussed changing the sample frame to remove the low quality stratum but rejected this idea because we would no longer have inference to the entire study area. We next discussed combining strata as a way to reduce overall sample size requirements and decided to adjust the sample design in this way. We choose to combine the high- and medium-quality catchments into a single habitat class. We used the original random order to determine which catchments we would always revisit and adjusted (downward) the number of catchments per basin (26) that we would monitor annually with available base funds. Monitoring of the 14 remaining catchments is dependent on available funds and resources which can vary from year to year. The revised number of catchments per basin proposed for long-term monitoring is presented in table 2.

Table 2. Number of catchments per access class, habitat class, and basin sampling proposed for long-term monitoring from 2009 forward.

		Basins						
Access Class[1]	Habitat Class[2]	Northern Range	Yellow-stone	Madison-Gallatin	Snake-Henrys Fk	Grand Teton-north[3]	Grand Teton-south	Total catchments
		Catchments Monitored Every Year						
Far	Med_high	1	1	1	1	1	1	6
Far	Low	1	1	1	1	—	1	5
Close	Med_high	2	2	2	2	1	1	10
Close	Low	1	1	1	1	1	—	5
Total		5	5	5	5	3	3	26
		Monitored Catchments that are Dependent on Additional Funds						
Far[4]	Med_high	1	1	1	1	—	—	4
Close[4]	Med_high	2	2	2	2	1	1	10
Total		3	3	3	3	1	2	14

[1]Based on catchment distance < or > 4 km from a road.
[2]Based on the amount and type of wetlands in each catchment identified by the National Wetland Inventory.
[3]Grand Teton is in the Snake Basin; it was divided into north and south zones to achieve better spatial representation.
[4]Catchments to be monitored as second priority.

2.3 Amphibian surveys

Procedures for surveys are detailed in our draft protocol (Amphibian Monitoring Working Group 2008). Two-person field crews visit all potential amphibian breeding sites within the boundaries of the selected catchments. Surveys are conducted at all sites with suitable water, following standard amphibian visual encounter methodology (Thoms et al 1997). This entails walking the perimeters of water bodies and transects through shallow ponds and wetlands, and using long-handled dip-nets to sweep the water for amphibian larvae. To determine the presence of breeding populations, we search for life stages that indicate breeding has occurred: eggs, larvae, or recent metamorphs. Each field crew member surveys the site independently (dual observer method), to provide data on species detectability. Catchments are visited once per season. We attempt to time the surveys to occur within the optimal period for finding the larvae of all four species. The timing, however, is constrained by a variety of factors including grizzly bear (*Ursus arctos horribilis*) and other wildlife administrative closures, river crossings, and field crew availability.

Data collected in the field includes location (initially recorded with a Global Positioning System (GPS)) receiver, time spent searching, species observed (life stages, number of adult and juveniles and categorical estimates of larvae and metamorphs), weather, water temperatures, and habitat descriptors (Amphibian Monitoring Working Group 2008). Sites are documented with drawings on the initial visits and updated as necessary. Photo points are set up on the initial visit and photos are re-taken each year. To save time and money in 2008 given the increased number of targeted catchments, we discontinued our former practices of collecting pH and conductivity and documenting larvae with photos. Data were recorded with personal digital assistants (PDAs). Abbreviated field survey sheets were used as a backup; they include the site identifier, date and time of visit, observers, species/life stages observed, photo number, and site drawing (if needed). The PDAs were programmed using forms software (Pendragron Forms), and downloaded directly into a Microsoft Access database provided by USGS-ARMI and slightly modified for use in Grand Teton and Yellowstone as coordinated by the GRYN Data Manager. The relational database, containing multiple tables, is standardized for use in the Rocky Mountain Region by USGS-ARMI.

In 2008, surveys of catchments began on 19 June and ended on 4 August, and in 2009 surveys began on 12 June and ended on 30 July. Two 2-person field crews based at Lake in Yellowstone worked through the season each survey year. A third team composed of the field coordinator working with different individuals and volunteers as they became available also conducted catchment surveys. In addition, the USGS-ARMI provided a team of two people for 5-6 days each year, Yellowstone Fisheries and Aquatic Sciences crews completed surveys in three catchments in 2008, and the whitebark pine field crew completed one large catchment in a remote area of Yellowstone in 2009.

2.4 Potential breeding sites within catchments

To address Objective 2, we annually track the number of sites within target catchments that are potentially suitable for amphibian breeding. Snowpack of the preceding winter and weather conditions of spring and early summer strongly influence the number and persistence of surface water in seasonal wetlands and thus the number of potential breeding sites. By tracking the number of available breeding sites annually, we can attempt to identify to what extent habitat loss due to drought or climate change affects amphibian occurrence. Methods for assessing annual variation in potential breeding sites and incorporating this factor in site-level occupancy are currently under development (Gould 2010).

On the initial visits to catchments, field crews hiked to all National Wetland Inventory (NWI) areas with attribute codes that indicate the presence of ephemeral or permanent, shallow surface water (see protocol for details; Amphibian Monitoring Working Group 2008). At these wetland sites, the crews made one of three determinations: site has water and is suitable for survey as a potential amphibian breeding site (suitable); site lacks sufficient surface water but may be suitable in other years or conditions (potential); site is dry or too shallow, and there are no indicators that a suitable wetland is present under any conditions (not suitable). The protocol guided the crews in the decision process for defining, classifying, and assigning identifying numbers to sites. In subsequent years, field crews visit the sites that were classified as suitable (surveyed) as well as those deemed potential, but not those that were categorized as not suitable. Any new suitable sites that are encountered, including newly created sites or ones that were missed in previous visits, are also surveyed. Records are kept in the database of all sites visited, including the rationale for not conducting a survey (e.g., dry, too shallow, or inaccessible due to hazards such as thermal conditions or deep mud). The number of "new sites" is expected to be small, now that all catchments in the sampling scheme have received an initial visit. Site characterizations are sometimes switched from "potential" to "not suitable" with cumulative evidence that the site is not capable of holding adequate surface water to constitute breeding habitat.

2.5 Boreal toad monitoring

Boreal toads are monitored with a dual frame, including surveys in the selected catchments as per Objective 1, and surveys of previously identified toad breeding areas (from here on called P-I areas). Based on a comprehensive list of locations compiled from previous amphibian databases and records, 42 toad breeding areas (some containing multiple breeding sites) have been found in Yellowstone and Grand Teton (fig. 4 and appendix 1), including the catchments and P-I areas. As of 2009, six known toad breeding areas have been found within the 40 catchments selected for long-term monitoring under Objective 1. The remaining 36 P-I areas were identified during other amphibian survey projects or opportunistically over the past decade. Surveys of P-I areas are not covered by current funding levels, given that the catchment surveys (Objective 1) have higher priority. In 2008 and 2009, as in previous years, a subset of the P-I areas was surveyed for toad breeding by an experienced volunteer team who has worked with us on amphibian monitoring in Yellowstone since 1996 (Char and Dave Corkran), and by the field coordinator on a time-available basis.

To select a subset of P-I areas for monitoring in 2008, random numbers were assigned to each area, with areas assembled into eight groups based on three access classes and two status classes (see appendix 1). The targets for 2008 included 12 randomly selected areas from the "easy/major" class, and 4 from the remaining classes, excepting the "far" class, which is not attainable with our resources. Monitoring consisted of conducting visual encounter surveys at the known breeding sites. The dual observer method was not used. Data were collected on paper forms and compiled by the field coordinator with donated time. Surveys were conducted at 16 P-I areas in 2008 and 17 P-I areas in 2009.

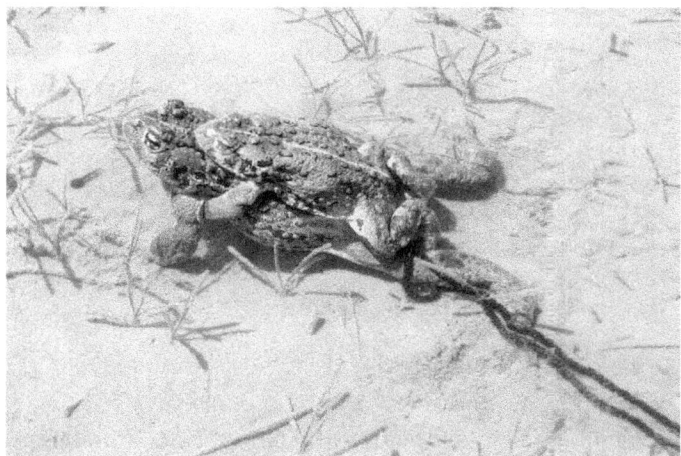

Figure 3. Boreal toads breeding at Indian Pond in Yellowstone National Park

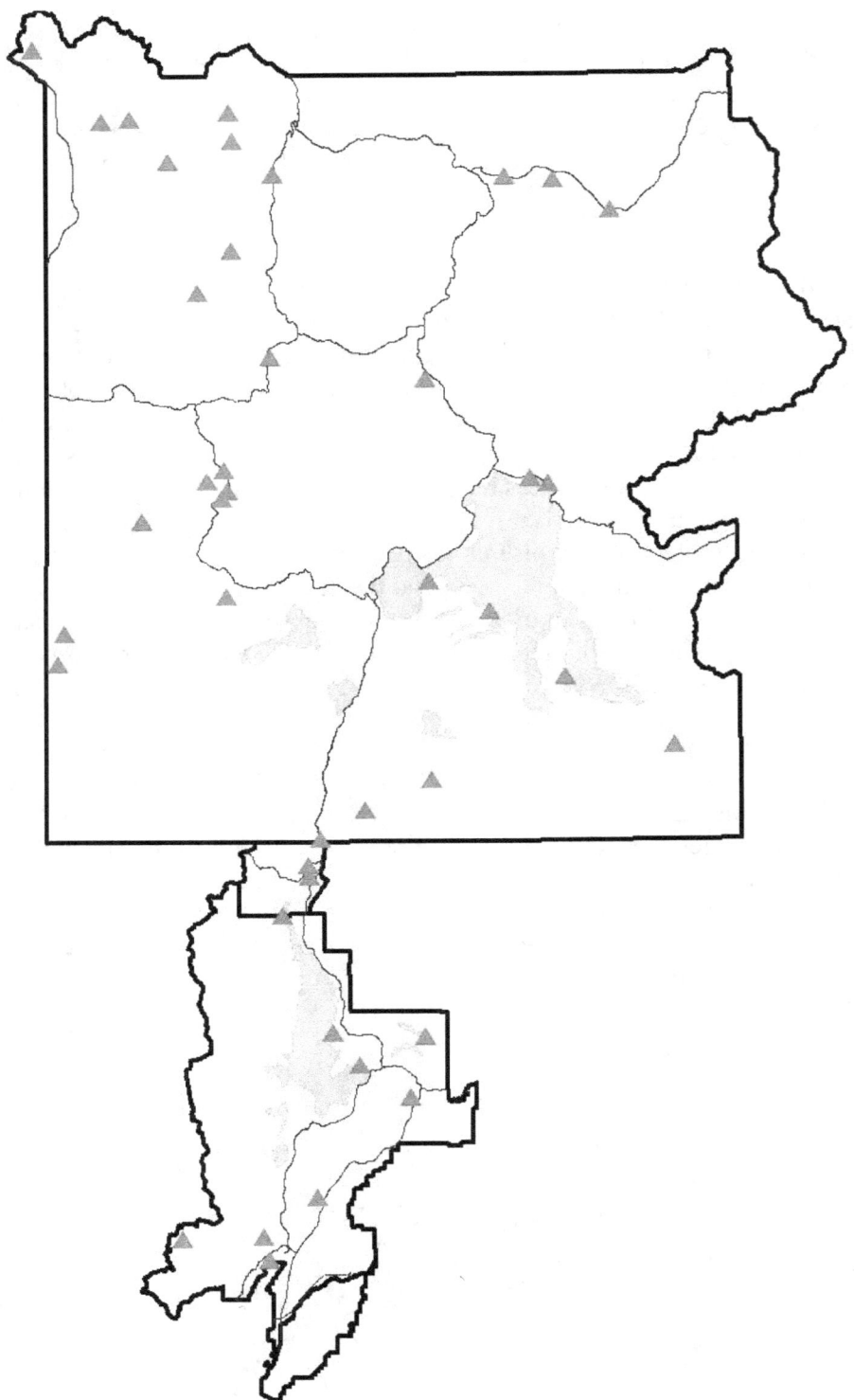

Figure 4. Boreal toad breeding areas in Yellowstone and Grand Teton (triangles). Breeding sites within 500 m of each other have been clustered as "toad breeding areas" for monitoring. A total of 42 breeding areas have been identified to date, six of which occur within catchments selected for the long-term monitoring project.

2.6 Data analysis

Proportion of area occupied (PAO) modeling provides a statistical framework for assessing changes in species occurrence (MacKenzie et al. 2002; Royle and Nichols 2003; MacKenzie et al. 2006). The proportion of area occupied (PAO) approach we are using provides a measure that: (1) explicitly enables estimation of local extinctions and colonization of sites; (2) accounts for imperfect detectability of individual species; (3) enables estimation of confidence intervals; (4) is comparable across sites; and (5) has become a widely accepted approach for reliable estimates of occupancy (MacKenzie et al. 2006). Information from repeated observations at sample units is used to estimate detectability and adjust occupancy rates for imperfect detection (failure to observe a species that is actually present). Occupancy models allow for analysis of covariates potentially affecting occupancy (e.g., habitat class), and covariates affecting detectability (e.g., observer). The analysis philosophy is optimization, based on evaluating which model or set of models best explains observed patterns, rather than the elimination of models using hypotheses testing. Model selection is accomplished using information theoretic methods, specifically Akaike's information criterion (AIC) differences and weights, to evaluate the models.

Occupancy will be assessed at two levels: catchments (portions of watersheds containing multiple potential sites) and sites (individual ponds or wetlands). The catchment level approximates the "breeding population" identified by ARMI as the feasible target for monitoring amphibian population trends in national parks. Occupancy at this level will be the major vehicle for meeting the goal of determining if amphibians are declining, stable, or increasing in Grand Teton and Yellowstone. Occupancy at the site level is a lower-scale measure that will allow one to investigate the importance of site-specific and survey-specific variables affecting detection probability and occupancy at individual wetlands.

For this report, we conducted a provisional analysis of occupancy at the catchment level using one of the best supported models from the 2007 data analysis which combined the habitat strata into two groups (high quality + medium quality, and low quality) and considered detection rates to be constant among strata. This was the best model in 2007 for Columbia spotted frogs and tiger salamanders, and the second best model for boreal chorus frogs (see appendix II in Patla and Gould 2009). The assumption that this model adequately fits the 2008 and 2009 data is tenuous, and we emphasize the provisional nature of the results reported here.

To estimate occupancy at the target population level (including Grand Teton and Yellowstone), we combined the stratum-level estimates according to design-based methodology (e.g., Thompson 1992) in a weighted mean (weighted by the number of catchments in each habitat class; Gould 2008).

The weighted average and variance were computed as:

$$\bar{\psi} = \sum_{h=1}^{L} \frac{N_h}{N} \hat{\psi}_h$$

where h indexes each stratum, and N_h is the stratum size such that

$$\sum_{h=1}^{L} N_h = N.$$

The estimated variance is

$$V\hat{a}r(\overline{\hat{\psi}}) = \sum_{h=1}^{L} \left(\frac{N_h}{N}\right)^2 \left(\frac{N_h - n_h}{N_h}\right) V\hat{a}r(\hat{\psi}_h)$$

where n_h represents the number of catchments sampled from stratum h and $V\hat{a}r(\hat{\psi}_h)$ is the square of the estimated standard error for stratum h.

To extract data from the amphibian database for the analysis, we used an interface tool provided by ARMI, which includes a PAO File Generator. For occupancy and detectability estimates, we used the program Presence 2.3 (Hines 2006). Each species was assessed separately.

2.7 Potential breeding site data analysis

Central to understanding amphibian occupancy dynamics is the assessment of how wetlands change from year to year. Methods for combining occupancy and habitat data to determine how amphibian occupancy changes as a function of available wetlands are under development (McKenzie et al. 2006, Gould 2010). Currently, we simply track the number and percentage of sites that are suitable or potential breeding habitat (e.g., dry or too shallow to support amphibian breeding) each year so that data are available for future analysis.

2.8 Boreal toad data analysis

The dual frame analysis methods needed to combine results of catchment and P-I area surveys have not been developed due to funding limitations. In this report we summarize results of the two sampling approaches separately for boreal toads for both 2008 and 2009 survey years.

3 Results

3.1 Catchments sampled and breeding sites surveyed

In 2008, we sampled a total of 40 catchments, 32 of which were in Yellowstone and 8 in Grand Teton (tables 2 and 3). Four catchments were visited for the first time in 2008; these were in the low-quality habitat stratum and were not previously sampled due to our earlier sampling design, which called for sampling catchments in this stratum every five years. Relative to 2007, occupancy data were collected in seven additional catchments in 2008: the four low-quality habitat catchments that were not previously surveyed; two low-quality catchments that were surveyed in 2005 and 2006 but not in 2007, and one catchment in which all sites were either dry or inaccessible in 2007. A total of 435 wetland sites were visited (334 in Yellowstone, 101 in Grand Teton). Of these, 356 sites were suitable, accessible, and subject to survey for amphibian breeding (281 in Yellowstone, 75 in Grand Teton).

In 2008, it took approximately 87 field days (two people working about 10 hours per day) to accomplish the work, including travel time within the parks, surveys, and data entry; but not including training. Field time per catchment varied from 1 to 6 days, with an average of 2.3 days per catchment. Donated field assistance for catchment monitoring in 2008 is estimated to be the rough equivalent of $3,500 in direct costs, a very substantial benefit for the project.

In 2009, we sampled a total of 37 catchments, 29 of which were in Yellowstone and 8 in Grand Teton. A total of 362 sites were visited (276 in Yellowstone, 86 in Grand Teton). Of these, 307 sites were suitable, accessible, and subject to survey for amphibian breeding (234 in Yellowstone; 73 in Grand Teton). Relative to 2008, occupancy data were collected in 3 fewer catchments due to funding limitations. In 2009 it took approximately 79 field days and 1,870 hours, including hired field crews and donated assistance from other programs to accomplish this work. To complete all 40 catchments, an additional 8 field-crew days (approx. 160 hours) were needed.

We found active breeding sites (identified by the presence of eggs, larvae, or recent metamorphs) of four species in both parks (table 3) each year. No leopard frogs or bullfrogs were found.

Note that effort levels and the set of targeted catchments varied over the years for the data depicted in table 3, which affects the number of sites surveyed and breeding sites found. To provide survey results obtained with consistent effort, table 4 provides data from the set of 31 catchments that were surveyed in 2007, 2008, and 2009 (three consecutive years).

Table 3. Results of amphibian monitoring in 2005–2009. Total numbers of catchments and sites surveyed per basin, and the number of catchments and sites containing breeding sites for amphibian species.

	Catchments surveyed	Sites surveyed	Tiger salamander		Boreal toad		Chorus frog		Spotted frog	
			Catchments	Sites	Catchments	Sites	Catchments	Sites	Catchments	Sites
2005[1]										
Northern Range	4	10	2	2	1	1	3	5	1	3
Yellowstone	2	26	0	0	0	0	1	3	2	6
Madison-Gallatin	2	16	0	0	0	0	2	2	1	2
Snake-Henrys Fk	4	31	1	1	0	0	4	9	3	9
Grand Teton	3	38	1	2	1	3	1	3	2	3
Total	15	121	4	5	2	4	11	22	9	23
2006										
Northern Range	6	24	5	10	3	3	4	9	5	7
Yellowstone	5	40	0	0	1	1	2	11	4	6
Madison-Gallatin	6	71	1	1	0	0	5	30	4	13
Snake-Henrys Fk	8	65	0	0	0	0	4	16	5	15
Grand Teton	7	62	3	8	1	4	4	16	4	13
Total	32	262	9	19	5	8	19	82	22	54
2007										
Northern Range	7	22	4	10	2	2	4	8	2	3
Yellowstone	7[2]	46	0	0	0	0	2	5	5	7
Madison-Gallatin	6	46	1	1	0	0	5	25	4	13
Snake-Henrys Fk	7	42	1	1	0	0	5	12	5	12
Grand Teton	7	65	3	5	1	2	3	14	4	11[3]
Total	34[2]	221	9	17	3	4	19	64	20	46[3]

[1] 2005 was a pilot year in which only a portion of the selected catchments were monitored.
[2] One of these catchments had no suitable sites in 2007.
[3] Number of spotted frog sites is corrected from the previous report (Patla and Gould 2009); 11 breeding sites were found in the Grand Teton unit and 46 total sites in 2007.

14

Table 3. (continued)

	Catchments surveyed	Sites surveyed	Tiger salamander		Boreal toad		Chorus frog		Spotted frog	
			Catchments	Sites	Catchments	Sites	Catchments	Sites	Catchments	Sites
2008										
Northern Range	8	35	6	9	2	3	6	25	4	8
Yellowstone	8	84	2	6	1	3	4	28	6	13
Madison-Gallatin	8	87	1	1	0	0	6	33	5	18
Snake-Henrys Fk	8	75	1	1	0	0	7	29	6	13
Grand Teton	8	75	4	9	2	2	5	18	4	12
Total	40	356	14	26	5	8	28	123	25	64
2009										
Northern Range	7	30	4	9	2	3	4	14	3	6
Yellowstone	8	80	1	1	1	2	4	25	6	10
Madison-Gallatin	7	60	0	0	0	0	6	24	4	11
Snake-Henrys Fk	7	64	0	0	0	0	6	18	5	7
Grand Teton	8	73	2	4	1	2	5	19	3	14
Total	37	307	7	14	4	7	25	100	21	48

Table 4. Results of monitoring in 31 catchments that were surveyed each year, 2007, 2008, and 2009: number of sites surveyed, sites visited but found dry or too shallow for amphibian breeding, and number of active breeding sites per species in this set of catchments.

Year	Sites Surveyed	Potential sites, dry or too shallow	Tiger Salamander sites	Boreal Toad sites	Chorus Frog sites	Spotted Frog sites
2007	195	141	13	3	54	35
2008	292	26	24	7	104	47
2009	283	21	14	7	99	45

3.2 Amphibian occupancy and detectability

Provisional catchment occupancy rates in 2008 ranged from 0.06 (SE=0.02) for boreal toads to 0.49 (SE=0.10) for boreal chorus frogs (table 5). In 2009, provisional catchment occupancy rates ranged from 0.05 (SE=0.02) for boreal toads to 0.47 (SE=0.10) for boreal chorus frogs (table 6). Detectability rates were high and consistent between years. Note that, as described in Methods, the scarcity of boreal toad occurrence within the selected catchments led to recognition of the need for supplementary monitoring of this species, with results described in section 3.3 below.

Site occupancy rates are not provided in this report because analysis methodology at this level is still under study (e.g., Gould 2010). Site occupancy calculation and modelling is challenging for three main reasons: sites are clustered and not independent, the number of suitable sites varies annually (see Section 3.3 below), and the total number of sites (unlike catchments) in the study area is unknown.

Table 5. Provisional catchment-level occupancy and detection rates from 2008 monitoring data. Occupancy estimates were calculated using a model that allowed occupancy to vary by habitat strata (high+medium and low) and assumed constant detectability across strata.

Species	Occupancy	Standard error	Detection rate	Standard error
Tiger salamander	0.16	0.03	0.88	0.07
Boreal chorus frog	0.49	0.10	0.96	0.03
Col spotted frog	0.45	0.08	0.96	0.02
Boreal toad	0.06	0.02	1.00	0.00

Table 6. Provisional catchment-level occupancy and detection rates from 2009 monitoring data. Occupancy estimates were calculated using a model that allowed occupancy to vary by habitat strata (high+medium and low) and assumed constant detectability across strata.

Species	Occupancy	Standard error	Detection rate	Standard error
Tiger salamander	0.09	0.03	0.88	0.12
Boreal chorus frog	0.47	0.10	0.96	0.03
Col spotted frog	0.42	0.10	0.95	0.04
Boreal toad	0.05	0.02	1.00	0.00

3.3 Potential Breeding Sites

In 2008, we visited 435 sites, including 65 new sites, with surveys conducted at 356 sites (table 9). New sites were added due to the increase in the number of low-quality catchments surveyed, and also due to wetter conditions in 2008 compared to the previous 2 years. Some previously-visited sites could not be reached due to high, unfordable rivers in 2008: seven sites in the Bechler catchment and 12 sites in the Thorofare catchment.

In 2009, we visited 362 sites, including 5 new sites, with surveys conducted at 307 sites. Crews were able to reach sites across the Bechler River in 2009, but not across the Thorofare River. The reduced number of catchments sampled in 2009 resulted in the loss of 37 sites that were surveyed in 2008. In both years, some sites were changed from 'potential' to 'not suitable' as it became clear that these sites will not support sufficient water even with wetter conditions.

Variation in the proportion of sites deemed suitable for breeding ('% of suitable sites' in table 9) reflects the dynamic nature of seasonal wetlands. The proportion of suitable sites increased sharply in 2008 and compared to 2009, presumably reflecting wetter conditions. Analysis of the relationship among climate patterns, site suitability, and amphibian occupancy is in progress.

Table 9. Tally of site visits and surveys per year, 2006–2009.

Year	Sites visited	New sites	No potential	Sites deemed suitable for breeding amphibians	% of suitable sites	Potential, not surveyed because dry or too shallow	Potential, not surveyed due to other reasons
2006	439	171	93	262	75.7	73	11
2007	421	95	37	221	57.6	157	6
2008	434	65	41	356	90.6	29	8
2009	362	5	27	307	91.6	22	6

Notes:
- *Sites visited:* All sites visited by field crews, including sites not surveyed; does not include sites that could not be reached due to high rivers or other conditions.
- *New sites:* On the initial visit to a catchment, all sites are new. Thereafter, this refers to sites that were missed in previous years and newly created sites.
- *No potential:* Field crew determined this was not likely to be suitable for amphibian breeding, even with wetter conditions.
- *Sites deemed suitable for breeding:* Conditions appeared to be suitable for breeding; crew conducted survey. This tally includes *new, suitable sites.*
- *% of suitable sites:* Proportion of sites suitable for breeding (Suitable sites / [Sites visited – no potential] = % of suitable sites). The proportion should increase in wet years, and decline in dry years.
- *Potential, not surveyed:* Reason for not conducting a survey at a site is either because it is too dry or shallow or for other reasons (e.g., flooded by high river water or a beaver dam breach, inaccessible, or hazardous)

3.4 Boreal toads, supplementary monitoring

Toad breeding (eggs, tadpoles, or recent metamorphs) was confirmed at 15 of the 16 previously identified (P-I) toad breeding areas that were surveyed in 2008 (appendix I). The only surveyed P-I area with no toad breeding detected in 2008 was at a site where breeding has not been confirmed since 1999. The year 2008 apparently provided excellent conditions for toad breeding; one of the areas found occupied in 2008 had not supported toad reproduction since 1997, and another not since 2002. In 2009, toad breeding (eggs, tadpoles, or recent metamorphs) was confirmed at 12 of the 17 previously identified (P-I) toad breeding areas surveyed (appendix I). One new probable toad breeding site was discovered in Grand Teton.

3.5 Amphibian disease surveillance monitoring

In 2009, we collaborated with the Yellowstone National Park Amphibian Disease Surveillance Program (St-Hilaire et al. 2009). No significant mortality events were found by the monitoring project field crews in 2009, but a die-off of boreal toad tadpoles was found near the south entrance of Yellowstone during informal toad monitoring (see St-Hilaire 2009). An amphibian disease database has been compiled for the GYE, including observed amphibian mortality over the past decade and diagnostic records for approximately 200 specimens that were submitted for analysis. The database and further investigation of disease has the potential to inform the amphibian monitoring program. Preliminary assessment of the database indicates that viral disease (ranavirus) may be widespread in the GYE, with confirmed or presumptive outbreaks of this disease detected in all four species.

4 Discussion

In 2008, we completed surveys in all 40 catchments designated by the project's sampling design, while in 2009 the effort was scaled down to 37 catchments due to funding constraints. In 2008 and 2009, in contrast to the previous two years (2006 and 2007), all ten selected catchments in the low quality habitat category were surveyed, following new recommendations (Patla and Gould 2009). These catchments, which have smaller amounts of wetlands relative to the high-medium habitat quality category, are more representative of the entire study area. They comprise 67% (N = 2245) of all catchments in the sample frame containing wetlands (N = 3370) (appendix II in Patla and Gould 2009). Amphibian breeding occurrence is apparently low in this type of catchment; we found two species (boreal chorus frogs and Columbia spotted frogs) in 3 of 10 catchments in both years (2008 and 2009). Breeding by tiger salamanders and boreal toads was not detected at all in this low quality habitat category. The apparent scarcity of amphibian breeding over the majority of the study area has important implications. One is the need to qualify our previously statements that 3 amphibian species (Columbia spotted frogs, boreal chorus frogs, and tiger salamanders) may be considered common and widespread in Yellowstone and Grand Teton; rather, their occurrence should be seen as dependent on limited and unevenly distributed suitable wetland breeding habitat. Another matter to consider is that our sampling effort and the number of detections may be too small to enable meaningful analyses for the majority of the area under study, as cautioned in the Protocol (Amphibian Monitoring Working Group 2008, 13). Detecting a population decline with respect to low quality habitat in Yellowstone and Grand Teton could be problematic with such sparse data, particularly for tiger salamanders.

Following five or more years of below-normal precipitation in the GYE, amphibians and their habitat appeared to respond vibrantly to the wet winter and spring of 2008. In the set of 31 catchments that were surveyed consistently 2007 through 2009, we found 97 additional suitable wetland sites in 2008 compared to 2007, an increase of 50% (table 4). In this set of catchments, all amphibian species demonstrated sharp increases in the raw number of detected active breeding sites between 2007 and 2008; particularly boreal chorus frog sites, which showed a 93% increase. In 2009, a second year of abundant precipitation but with a cold spring that delayed snow melt, the numbers of suitable sites and active breeding sites were relatively stable except for a drop in tiger salamander breeding sites. Informal supplementary monitoring of known boreal toad breeding areas found a pattern similar to that of tiger salamanders, with an increase of active breeding sites in 2008, and a decrease in 2009. Possible weather-related hypotheses for the drop in active breeding sites in 2009 are that cold weather in May and June inhibited breeding or caused high mortality of eggs and larvae for these two species, or that adult females were unable to produce clutches in consecutive years. This snapshot of an observed increase between 2007 and 2008/2009 demonstrates the resilience of the region's native amphibians, which have a suite of characteristics that allows them to respond to improved moisture conditions with increased breeding efforts. It also, however, suggests their vulnerability if climate change results in extended periods of unrelieved drought, shrinking wetlands, and larger proportions of available water diverted for human uses. We hope to investigate the connections of climate change, seasonal weather fluctuations, and amphibian response in the coming year.

The discussion above is based on descriptive observation in a subset of catchments, rather than a statistical assessment relevant to the entire study area. Also, catchment occupancy estimates reported for 2008 and 2009 in Section 3.2 are provisional and should not be compared to the 2007 results, which were based on more refined modeling procedures (Patla and Gould 2009). A manuscript presenting multi-year analysis of occupancy data collected between 2006 and 2008 is in preparation, and/or will be reported in the 2010 annual report.

The utility of long-term monitoring and a sampling design that provides inference to the parks was illustrated by a publication in a major scientific journal heralding "severe declines in 4 once-common amphibian species native to Yellowstone," caused by climate warming (McMenamin et al. 2008). The study compared presence/absence data from 1992–93 (Hill and Moore 1994) to data collected 2006-2008. Review of the paper and the historical data set by the Yellowstone-Grand Teton Monitoring Project PI's and field coordinator (published as a letter to the journal, Patla et al. 2009) found that the research was limited to a small area of Yellowstone, and that it failed to demonstrate the loss of populations due to its confounding of "populations" with sites found occupied by even one adult amphibian within dispersal distance of other sites. In their reply to the letter, the authors of the journal paper defended their study but concluded "[t]he uncertainties that Patla et al. identify further emphasize the need for long-term monitoring of the type conducted by their team." (McMenamin et al. 2009). Without long-term monitoring designed to encompass the size of the parks, complexity of habitats, and the response of breeding populations to environmental fluctuations, it is difficult to distinguish local changes from significant declines, or to interpret the scale of changes and their causes.

5 Literature Cited

Alford, R.A., P.M. Dixon, and J.H.K. Pechmann. 2001. Global amphibian population declines. *Nature* 414: 449–500.

Amphibian Monitoring Working Group. 2008. Cooperative Amphibian Monitoring Protocol for the Greater Yellowstone Network. National Park Service, Greater Yellowstone Network. Bozeman, MT. Collins, J. P., and A. Storfer. 2003. Global amphibian declines: sorting the hypotheses. *Diversity and Distributions* 9: 89–98.

Corn, P. S., M. J. Adams, W. A. Battaglin, A. L. Gallant, D. L. James, M. Knutson, C. Langtimm, and J. R. Sauer. 2005a. Amphibian Research and Monitoring Initiative–Concepts and implementation. US Geological Survey Scientific Investigations Report 2005–5015.

Corn, P. S., B. R. Hossack, E. Muths, D. A. Patla, C. R. Peterson, and A. L. Gallant. 2005b. Status of amphibians on the Continental Divide: surveys on a transect from Montana to Colorado, USA. *Alytes* 22 (3–4): 85–94.

Crother, B.I. (Committee chair) 2008. Scientific and standard English names of amphibians and reptiles of North America north of Mexico, with comments regarding confidence in our understanding. 6th edition. Herpetological Circular No. 37, published January 2008. Society for the Study of Amphibians and Reptiles. http://www.ssarherps.org.

Gascon C., J. P. Collins, R. D. Moore, D. R. Church, J. E. McKay, and J. R. Mendelson (editors). 2007. Amphibian Conservation Action Plan Proceedings: IUCN/SSC Amphibian Conservation Summit 2005. The World Conservation Union (IUCN), Gland, Switzerland.

Gould, W. R. 2008. Evaluation of sampling designs and analysis of data collected by the Greater Yellowstone Network Vital Signs monitoring program. National Park Service, Greater Yellowstone Network Unpublished Report, Bozeman, MT.

Gould, W.R. 2010. Multi-scale occupancy modeling of breeding amphibians for the Greater Yellowstone Network Vital Signs Monitoring Program. National Park Service, Greater Yellowstone Network Unpublished Report, Bozeman, MT.

Green, D. M. 1997. Perspectives on amphibian population declines: defining the problem and searching for answers. Pages 291–308 *in* Herpetological Conservation, Vol. I. Amphibians in decline. Canadian studies of a global problem, D. M. Green, editor. Society for the Study of Amphibians and Reptiles, St. Louis, MO.

Hill S. R., R. E. Moore. 1994. Herpetological survey in the northern range of Yellowstone National Park. Investigator's Annual Reports, Yellowstone National Park.

Hines, J. E. 2006. PRESENCE2- Software to estimate patch occupancy and related parameters. USGS-PWRC. Available from http://www.mbr-pwrc.usgs.gov/software/presence.html.

Houlahan, J. E., C. S. Findley, B. R. Schmidy, A. H. Meyer, and S. L. Kuzmin. 2000. Quantitative evidence for global amphibian declines. *Nature* 404: 752–755.

Jean, C. A.M. Schrag, R.E. Bennetts, R. Daley, E.A. Crowe, S. O'Ney. 2005. Vital Signs Monitoring Plan for the Greater Yellowstone Network. National Park Service, Greater Yellowstone Network, Bozeman MT. 107 pp plus appendices.

Koch, E. D., and C. R. Peterson. 1995. Amphibian and reptiles of Yellowstone and Grand Teton National Parks. University of Utah Press, Salt Lake City, UT.

MacKenzie, D. I., J. D. Nichols, G. B. Lachman, S. Droege, J. A. Royle, and C. A. Langtimm. 2002. Estimating site occupancy when detection probabilities are less than one. *Ecology* 83(8): 2248–2255.

MacKenzie D. I., J. D. Nichols, J. A. Royle, K. H. Pollock, L. L. Bailey, and J. E. Hines. 2006. Occupancy estimation and modeling: Inferring patterns and dynamics of species occurrence. Academic Press, San Diego, CA.

McMenamin S. K., E. A. Hadly, C. K. Wright. 2008. Climatic change and wetland desiccation cause amphibian decline in Yellowstone National Park. *Proceedings of the National Academy of Sciences* 105:16988–16993.

McMenamin S. K., E. A. Hadly, C. K. Wright. 2009. Reply to Patla et al.: Amphibian habitat and populations in Yellowstone damaged by drought and global warming. *Proceedings of the National Academy of Sciences* 106:E23.

Muths, E., P.S. Corn, A.P.Pessier, D.E.Green. 2003. Evidence for disease-related amphibian decline in Colorado. *Biological Conservation* 110 (2003) 357–365.

Muths, E., D.S. Pilliod, and L.J. Livo. 2008. Distribution and environmental limitation of an amphibian pathogen in the Rocky Mountains, USA. *Biological Conservation* 141 (2008) 1484-1492.

Patla, D., C. R. Peterson, and R. Bennetts. 2007. Amphibian monitoring in the Greater Yellowstone Network, 2006 project report. National Park Service, Greater Yellowstone Network Unpublished Report, Bozeman, MT.

Patla D. A., C. R. Peterson, P. S. Corn. 2009. Amphibian decline in Yellowstone National Park. *Proceedings of the National Academy of Sciences* 106:E22.

Patla, D. A., and W. R. Gould. 2009. Amphibian monitoring in the Greater Yellowstone Network - project report 2007. Yellowstone and Grand Teton National Parks. Natural Resource Technical Report NPS/GRYN/NRTR—2009/151. National Park Service, Fort Collins, Colorado.

Royle, J. A., and J. D. Nichols. 2003. Estimated abundance from repeated presence-absence data or point counts. *Ecology* 84(3): 777–790.

Stuart. S. N., J. S. Chanson, N. A. Cox, B. E. Young, A. S. L. Rodrigues, D. L. Fischman, and R. W. Waller. 2004. Status and trends of amphibian declines and extinctions worldwide. *Science* 306: 1783–1786.

St-Hilaire, S., C. R. Peterson, and S. Corn. 2009. Yellowstone National Park Amphibian Disease Monitoring Program. Project Proposal, Pocatello, Idaho.

St-Hilaire, S. 2009. Yellowstone National Park Amphibian Disease Monitoring Program. Year 1 Report. Unpublished Report, Pocatello, Idaho.

Thompson, S. K. 1992. Sampling. Wiley, New York, NY.

Thoms, C., C. C. Corkran, and D. H. Olson. 1997. Basic amphibian survey for inventory and monitoring in lentic habitats. In Sampling Amphibians in Lentic Habitats. D.H. Olson, W.P. Leonard, and R.B. Bury, editors. Northwest Fauna 4. Society for Northwestern Vertebrate Biology, Olympia, WA.

Wake, D. B, and V. T. Vredenburg. 2008. Are we in the midst of the sixth mass extinction? A view from the world of amphibians. *Proceedings of the National Academy of Science* 105: 11466–11473.

Appendix I: Boreal toad breeding areas

Population ID code	Access	Active breeding in 2009	Toad life stage found in 2009	Toad life stage found in 2008	Toad life stage found in 2007	Single or multiple breeding sites	Major or minor breeding site	Year of last toad breeding record	Year that area was last checked for toad breeding	General location
G1	Easy	yes	L	L,M,A	L, M	multiple	major	2009	2009	Flagg Ranch
G2	Easy	not checked	--	E,L,A	E,L,M	multiple	major	2008	2008	Snake River pit
G3	Day	not checked	--	--	--	multiple	major	2006	2006	Snake River above Jackson Lake
G4	Easy	yes	L	L,M	L, M,A	multiple	major	2009	2009	Colter Bay
G5*	Easy	yes	L, J	L,J,A	L,M	multiple	major	2009	2009	Willow Flats
G6	Day	not checked	--	--	L,M	multiple	major	2007	2007	Snake River downstream Moran
G7	Easy	checked too early & too late, not included in tally for '09	M (N=3)	L,M	L,M,J,A	multiple	major	2008	2008	Schwabacker Landing
G8	Easy	not checked	--	--	0	single	minor	2004	2007	Whitegrass Ranch
G9	Easy	not checked	--	--	0	single	minor	2004	2007	Snake River Moose-Wilson Rd
G10*	Day	no	0	L	--	single	minor	2008	2009	Death Canyon
G11	Easy	yes	M	--	--	single	minor	2009	2009	Two Ocean Lake
Y1	Day	no	0	L	0	single	minor	2008	2009	Daly Creek ponds
Y2	Day	no	0	L,J,A	L,J,M	single	major	2008	2009	Fan Creek
Y3	Remote	not checked	--	--	--	multiple	major	1999	1999	East Fan Creek
Y4	Remote	not checked	--	--	--	single	minor	2002	2002	Fawn Pass
Y5	Day	not checked	--	--	L,M	single	major	2007	2007	Fawn Lake
Y6*	Remote	not checked	--	L,J/A	L	single	major	2008	2008	Cache Lake
Y7	Easy	yes	L	L,A	L	multiple	major	2009	2009	Swan Flats
Y8	Easy	no	0	0	0	single	minor	1999	2008	Lamar Valley
Y9*	Day	yes	E,L,J/A	0	L,J/A	single	major	2009	2009	Crystal Bench

Population ID code	Access	Active breeding in 2009	Toad life stage found in 2009	Toad life stage found in 2008	Toad life stage found in 2007	Single or multiple breeding sites	Major or minor breeding site	Year of last toad breeding record	Year that area was last checked for toad breeding	General location
Y10	Easy	not checked	--	--	L,A	single	major	2007	2007	Soda Butte Cr
Y12	Remote	not checked	--	--	--	multiple?	minor	2001	2001	Duck Cr
Y13	Easy	yes	L	E,L	L,J	multiple	major	2009	2009	Gibbon Meadow
Y14	Easy	yes	L,J,A	L,A	L,J,A	multiple	major	2009	2009	Alum Creek
Y15	Remote	not checked	--	--	--	single	minor	2004	2004	Buffalo Meadow
Y16	Day	no	0	L	0	single	minor	2008	2009	Fairy Cr
Y17	Easy	yes	L	L	L,M	multiple	major	2009	2009	Firehole Lake Dr
Y18	Easy	no	0	--	0	single	minor	2005?	2009	Mary Mtn trail
Y19	Easy	yes	L	L	L,J	multiple	major	2009	2009	Tangled Cr
Y20	Easy	yes	E,L,A	E,L,J,A	E,L,M,J,A	single	major	2009	2009	Indian Pond
Y21	Remote	not checked	--	--	--	multiple	major	2002	2002	Boundary Cr
Y22	Remote	not checked	--	--	--	single	major	2002	2002	Boundary Cr
Y23	Day	yes	L	L,A	L,M	multiple	major	2009	2009	Lone Star
Y24	Remote	not checked	--	--	--	not sure	?	?	2006	Breeze Pt
Y25	Remote	not checked	--	--	--	not sure	?	?	2006	Eagle Bay
Y26	Easy	yes	L,M	L,A	L,A	multiple	major	2009	2009	South Entrance
Y27	Day	yes	L	--	L	single	major	2009	2009	Snake River Hotsprings
Y28	Remote	not checked	--	--	--	multiple	major	2003	2003	Heart River
Y29*	Remote	yes	L,J/A	L	0	multiple	minor	2009	2009	Winter Cr
Y30	Remote	not checked	0	--	--	single	minor	2006	2006	Mountain Cr
Y31*	Easy	yes	L	L	--	multiple	major	2009	2009	Mary Bay
Y32	Remote	not checked	0	L,M	--	single	?	2008	2008	East side of Promontory

Notes: *ID code:* Population ID code assigned for easy reference and database use; *Access:* Easy = <2 km from roads; Day = hike to and survey in one day; Remote = backpacking needed, 2-5 days; *Toad Life Stage:* E = eggs; L = tadpoles; M = metamorph; J = juvenile (immature, probably 1-2 years old); A= adult; *Single or multiple breeding sites:* Toad eggs or tadpoles found in one or multiple distinct sites within the area; *Major or minor.* Minor means <100 tadpoles seen 1 year; Major means hundreds or thousands of tadpoles, usually seen multiple years

*Catchments selected for long-term monitoring